My First Friggin' Cookbook

Gary Capuano

I am dedicating this book in honor of my parents, Gary, and Joyce Capuano (nee Lattino) who were married for 49 years; without them, there would be no me. Mom worked her whole life and after the death of my father in 2020, returned to work after being retired for several years. She came out of a twenty-year retirement to work during the height of COVID to help her cousin, a physician. My father also worked his whole life and was retired for about twenty years before his untimely death. He passed away from an aortic dissection. He wanted to retire early and enjoy life since his father and brother couldn't do so. My paternal grandfather was a stone mason and was killed on the job when a wall collapsed on him just months before his retirement. My uncle Jack was also close to his retirement when he passed from an aortic dissection.

Mom and Dad would often do without so that I could enjoy myself and not struggle as they had to growing up. They put me through Catholic school and even paid for college loans even though I decided to drop out. They clothed me. They FED me. They instilled morals, manners, and religious beliefs in me. They taught me respect. They taught me that there are consequences for one's actions. They taught me what it means to be a family and showed me what true love is, showing love and support in good times and in bad.

Table of Contents

INTRODUCTION

I was born and raised in South Philadelphia, a 3rd generation Italian. My paternal grandparents came from Naples and my maternal grandparents came from Calabria and Monteroduni. South Philly was an area where many neighborhoods were dominated by one ethnicity and for the most part, still is. My childhood home was on the 1600 block of South Rosewood Street. This area was once dominated by the Italians. South Philadelphia in recent years has begun to change with the influx of millennials. Growing up there were corner bars, luncheonettes, bakeries, fruit stores, butcher shops, fish stores, shoemakers, pharmacies, and corner stores where you could buy groceries, cigarettes, bread, lunchmeat, vegetables, and even fresh fish. All were mom and pop businesses started from the ground up. In the 1970's there weren't many big-name retailers in the neighborhood. This was a time when we still had a huckster who came into the neighborhood in his box truck to peddle his fruits and vegetables. If you were short on money, you could run a tab. We also had a life insurance man who would come to the house monthly to collect on the bill and then there was the guy who sold clothes from his car. The pretzel guy would push his old, wooden cart through the neighborhood, selling his goods. There was a snow cone guy in the summer who worked from a cart too.

My parents told me when they were growing up in the 1950's that they had the milkman who would make deliveries of fresh milk in a glass bottle to their step. During my grandparents' time there was the Javelle water guy(bleach) who would deliver their product as well as a guy who would deliver coal so they could heat the house. Bond Bread would deliver fresh donuts and bread to the house. There was a blind guy who would sell brooms and another guy who sharpened knives and fixed umbrellas from his cart, right then and there. There was the waffle man who pushed a cart and made fresh waffles and put ice cream between the two halves and added powdered sugar.

Many of the small businesses I previously mentioned had specialty items that were homemade. They used recipes that were handed down from generation to generation. Food was made fresh and there were no preservatives. There was hardly anything used that came out of a can or a box, one of the reasons they probably lived longer.

Here is a list of some of the better <u>bakeries</u> (according to me and my family) in my neighborhood throughout the years:

- » Danny's, 9th & Federal (Best Pound cake)

- » Pixie's Bakery, 1400 Snyder Ave.

- » Flacco's, 8th St. between Wharton & Sears St. (known for tomato pie, also made donuts and bread)

- » Cimineri's, 16th & Morris St.-famous for Italian Cream cake

- » Oteri's, Broad & Morris St.

- » Tally Ann Bakery, 11th & Emily St.

- » Sarcone's, 9th & Catharine St.

- » Faragalli's, 13th & Reed St. (Brick oven)

- » Varallo's, 10th & Morris St.

- » Iannelli's, 1100 E. Passyunk Ave (tomato pie)

- » Isgro's, 9th & Christian St.

- » Cacia's, 15th & Ritner St.

- » Cosmi's, Iseminger & Oregon Ave. (great jelly donuts)

- » Masi Schaffer, 15th & Mifflin St. (Choc chip cake w/shaved chocolate)

- » Abruzzi's, 22nd & Jackson St.

- » Imperial Bakery, 1500 Moore St.

- » Termini's, 8th & Dickinson St.

- » Frangelli's, 9th & Ritner St.

The following is a list I compiled of our famous <u>sandwich shops</u> in our area:

- » John's Roast Pork, Swanson & Snyder Ave.

- » Tony Luke's, Front & Oregon Ave.

- » Steak a Roma, Passyunk & Tasker St.

- » Pat's, 9th & Wharton St.

- » Jim's-across from Pats on 9th St. (Geno's Steaks Jimmy Vento's father Jim, prior to Geno's)

- » Geno's, Passyunk & Wharton St.

- » Shanks-10th & Carpenter St. (sausage 'n peppers)

- » Frankie Cabanas, 18th & Passyunk Ave.

- » Johnny Barrel's, 18th & Sigel St.-(best veal cutlet sandwich, breaded w/lettuce 'n tomato and shake pepper)

Here's a list of <u>diners</u>:

- » Emil's, Broad & Moore St.

- » George's Diner, Broad & Snyder Ave.

- » Melrose, 15th & Passyunk Ave.

- » Oregon Diner, 4th & Oregon Ave.

- » Penrose, 20th & Penrose Ave.

Finally, here's a list of <u>restaurants</u>:

- » Ralph's, 9th & Catherine St.

- » Villa Di Roma, 9th & Carpenter St.

- » Fiore's, Passyunk & Morris St.

- » South Philly Bar and Grille, 12th & Mercy St.

- » Sam's Cobblestone, 12th & Moyamensing Ave.

- » Stroli's, Carlisle & Dickinson St.

- » Dante and Luigi's, 10th & Catherine St.

- » Mama Yolanda's, 8th & Fitzwater St.

- » Cent' Anni's, 7th & Fulton St.

- » The Saloon, 7th & Clymer St.

- » Frankie's Seafood, 11th & Tasker St.

- » Joseph's, Passyunk & Mifflin St.

- » Walt's Crabhouse, 2nd & Queen St.

- » Snockey's Seafood, 8th & South St (before they moved to 2nd & Washington Ave.)

- » Pesto, Broad & Mifflin St.

- » Io e tu, 9th & Greenwich St.

- » Tre Scalini, Passyunk & Mifflin St.

- » Palumbo's (weddings) and the Nostalgia Room (previously the CR Club) for affairs 8th & Catherine St.

- » St. Michael's Club-7th & Wharton St. (for mussels)

South Philly is also home to many Italian specialty stores. There is Di Bruno Brother's and Claudio's on South 9th St. in the Italian Market and the recently closed Mancuso's on East Passyunk Ave. We have Cannuli Italian Sausages, Maglio Sausage Company and Maggio Cheese.

As far back as I can remember, my parents and I always sat down as a family at the dinner table. Whatever my mom cooked was it for that night-no special dishes because I didn't "like" what she was making. Mom would have every major holiday at the house and cook for upwards of fifteen people, especially on Christmas Eve for the seven fish feast. Food seemed to bring us together as a family. Macaroni would be served on Sundays, Tuesday, Thursday and on Fridays too during Lent! There were always leftovers. In my family, food was used not only to nourish but to also to comfort. If one was sick, they were told to eat. Chicken soup, stracciatella soup, escarole soup (wedding soup) or some acini di Pepe. If someone passed away, there would almost always be a luncheon, not only to say thank you but to feed you. I saw my father buy sandwiches, pizza, pastries for staff at doctor's offices to thank them for helping. I wanted to write this book and share with you the recipes to some of my favorite dishes and treats that I grew up with. I hope you enjoy them.

Sweets

EASTER MEAT PIE

- 4 cups of flour
- 6 tablespoons of vegetable shortening melted
- 2 teaspoons baking powder
- pinch salt
- 2 large eggs for dough
- 1 cup of ice water is for dough

Filling is

- 3 pounds ricotta and 9 eggs
- 3 tablespoons of macaroni cheese

Beat eggs and ricotta with a hand mixer. Stir in meats by hand. Dump into pan. Put in 400° oven for 15 minutes and then 325° for 45 minutes. You'll have to get approximately 4 slices of a quarter of an inch thick prosciutto and 4 slices of ham and dice into very small chunks. Add the macaroni cheese. Take fat off of prosciutto. You can add a pound of sweet sausage -fry in oil ahead of time. You can also add hard-boiled egg after adding the eggs and cheese (along with the meats) after its mixed. Stir in by hand. Vegetable shortening the square pan. Make strips of 1-inch-wide dough-2 across and 2 diagonally.

This recipe gets you two pies.

RICOTTA PIE

- 3 lbs. ricotta
- 12 large eggs
- 3 cups of sugar for filling

Melt 1/2 butter stick, judge your flour-not too dry, not sticky. Beat 5 eggs. 2 backs (handle of teaspoon) of baking powder. 4 tablespoons of sugar. Put into mix master. Bake at 350° for one hour- you should cut strips of dough approximately 1 inch wide and put across and diagonally. Brush strips with egg. Spread vegetable shortening on a square pan.

SWEET BREAD

- 6 large eggs

- 6 cups of flour

- 2 cups of sugar

- 6 teaspoons of baking powder

- 2 teaspoons of salt

- 1/2 pound of butter -Do not melt

- 6 tablespoons anise seed

- tablespoon of vanilla

- 2 packs yeast Rise-two times (3 hours each time)

- 1 cup warm water

◊   Mix by hand.

◊   Bake for 25, 30 minutes at 350°

   *Always use large eggs

You must plat the dough and brush with egg wash. Add multicolor non pareils to top. Let it sit another hour before putting in oven. Put on cookie sheet with vegetable shortening.

EASTER BREAD

- make into loaves
- 6 large eggs
- 6 tablespoons of sugar
- 1 teaspoon of salt
- 6 tablespoons melted butter
- 5 to 6 cups of flour
- 2 packages of yeast
- 2 teaspoons of baking powder
- 1 cup of hot water (mix yeast in it)
- 1 tablespoon anise seed
- orange rind and half tsp anise oil

◊ Rise-two times (3 hours each time)

Mix well by hand. Rise. Punch down, rise again. In 2 hours, fix as a loaf. Grease pan with vegetable shortening.

Brush with egg wash. No non pareils. Small cut across middle, approximately 1/2 size of loaf. 375° oven for about 20, 30 minutes. Makes 3, 4 loaves.

RICE PUDDING

- 4 cups milk
- 10 tablespoons sugar
- 8 tablespoons regular Carolina rice
- Teaspoon vanilla extract

Combine ingredients into a pot. Sprinkle cinnamon and add 2 pats of butter while the rice cooks. Add golden raisins if you want. Cook on stovetop until it boils, then lower and cook for another 45 minutes to an hour. When done, beat 2 egg yolks in a dish, stir in real fast. Sprinkle with more cinnamon.

JEWISH APPLE CAKE

- 3 cups flour
- 2 cups sugar
- 3 teaspoons baking powder
- 4 large eggs
- 1 cup oil
- 1/2 cup of orange juice
- 2 1/2 teaspoons vanilla extract
- 4 apples diced, remove skin
- 2 teaspoons cinnamon
- 5 tablespoons sugar

Mix apples with cinnamon and sugar in separate bowl first. Start the mix. Pour half of the batter into pan (vegetable shortening) then add apples. Pour rest of batter and add the rest of the apples. Bake at 350° for 1 hr. 20 minutes.

CHEESECAKE WITH SOUR CREAM TOPPING

- 1/2 cup sugar

- 3–8-ounce blocks of cream cheese

- 1-14 ounce can evaporated milk

- 3 large eggs

- 1/4 cup lemon juice

- 1–8-ounce sour cream container (after cake is cooked)

- 3 tablespoons of sugar

- 1 teaspoon of vanilla

◊   Mix by hand.

◊   Preheat oven. Bake at 300° for 50-55 minutes

Mix all the ingredients (except the sour cream, vanilla and 3 tbsps. sugar) together with a mix master. Put in spring pan (vegetable shortening). Before you pour batter in, put tin foil across the bottom and on sides (just the outside). Place into a roasting pan. Fill roasting pan with boiling water for a few inches. This helps the cheesecake not to crack. After the cake is cooked, let cool. Smear the sour cream mixture across the top and put back into oven and bake at 425° for about 5 minutes when it forms a glaze.

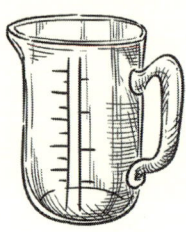

BLENDER CHEESECAKE

- 2-8oz. blocks of Philadelphia Cream Cheese

- 3/4 cup sugar

- 1 cup milk

- 4 large eggs

- 2 tablespoons corn starch

- 1 teaspoon vanilla extract

Put everything into blender for 5 minutes. Sprinkle with cinnamon. Grease a pan (pie dish) with vegetable shortening. Pour mix in. Bake at 325° for one hour.

CHOCOLATE CHIP CAKE

- yellow cake mix

- box of instant vanilla pudding

- 4 large eggs

- 1/2 cup milk

- 1/2 cup water

- 1/2 cup oil

Blend in mix master. Add 1/2 cup of chocolate jimmies (sprinkles)and 6 ounces of chocolate chips. Bake for 40 minutes at 350°.

PINEAPPLE CAKE

- 1/2 cup vegetable shortening
- 2 cups sugar
- 6 large eggs
- 2 1/2 cups flour
- 1 cup milk
- 3 teaspoons baking powder
- Mix master.

Coat bottom of pan with vegetable shortening. Now coat with brown sugar. Put round pineapple slices in and then pour batter on top. Bake at 350° for 1 hour.

SMALL 9TH STREET POUND CAKE

- 1/2 lb. butter- softened (leave out)
- 3 cups sugar
- Mix good with mix master.
- 6 large eggs, one at a time
- 3 cups flour
- 1/2 teaspoon baking powder
- 1 teaspoon vanilla extract

Pour into a bundt pan coated with vegetable shortening. Place into 325° oven for one hour and 15 minutes-don't preheat oven!

GARY'S BISCOTTI

- 1/4 cup olive oil

- 3/4 cup sugar

- 1 3/4 cup flour

- 2 teaspoons baking powder

- 1/4 teaspoon salt

- 2 large eggs

- 2 teaspoons vanilla extract

◊ Make into a loaf.

◊ Mix by hand.

Bake in 300° oven for 35 minutes. Reduce to 275°. Let it cool, maybe until warm. Put back after slicing into approximately one-inch slices for another 8-10 minutes then flip them over for maybe another 8-10 minutes.

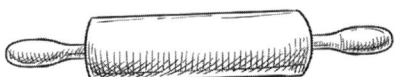

ALMOND SNOWBALLS

- 1 cup butter, softened
- 1/2 cup powdered sugar
- 1 teaspoon vanilla extract
- 2 1/4 cups flour
- 1/4 teaspoon salt
- 3/4 cup almonds, crushed

  *Can substitute with pecans. *

Cream butter in bowl. Add sugar. Mix well by hand. Stir in pan flour and salt. Stir in almonds. Shape into balls (approx. 1 inch diameter). Place onto greased baking pan. Bake at 350° for about 15 minutes. Remove from pan and roll into powdered sugar. Let cool and roll again.

BETTY COOKIES

- 6 large eggs
- 1 cup oil
- 2 tablespoons baking powder
- 1/2 lb. powdered sugar OR 2 cups powdered sugar

Mix by hand. Roll dough into approximately 1/2 in by approximately 6-inch-long piece and make cookie by twirling (like a poop emoji) or making into a plat. Bake in 375° oven for 10-12 minutes.

Mix powder sugar and milk into a paste. You can add food color. Dip cookie top into paste and let dry on wax paper. You can add almond or lemon extract into icing.

THUMB COOKIES

- 1/2 lb. butter, softened

- 1/2 cup sugar

- 2 egg yolks (save whites)

- 2 1/2 cups flour

- 2 tablespoons vanilla extract

Beat egg whites until foamy. Set aside.

Mix by hand. Roll dough into little balls. Press thumb into middle of ball. Add preserve of your choice into thumb print. Use tip of teaspoon. Put a small amount of egg white on top of preserve. Bake for 5-8 minutes at 350°.

FRUIT CAKE

- 2 cups flour

- 2 tablespoons baking powder

- 4 large eggs

- Get 16-ounce container of different color dried fruit.

- Use 2 teaspoons of allspice.

- 4 teaspoons of cinnamon

- Nuts (walnuts or pecans crushed) About a cup.

- Cup of golden raisins.

- 1 cup of sugar

- 1/2 cup of oil

Mix with hands and put into loaf pan. Line pan with wax paper or brown bag. Put vegetable shortening on the wax paper or bag. Pour in mix. Bake at 350° for 50-60 minutes. Let cool and then paint top of cake with clear corn syrup.

MACAROONS

- 4 egg whites
- 1/2 cup sugar
- dash salt
- 1/2 teaspoon almond extract
- 1 teaspoon vanilla extract
- 4 cups shredded, sweetened coconut

Mix with hands. Scoop mix with a teaspoon and place onto greased cookie sheet.

Bake at 350° for 20-25 minutes.

MARBLE CAKE

- 1/2 cup vegetable shortening OR 8 tablespoons
- 2 cups sugar
- 6 large eggs
- 3 cups flour
- 3 teaspoons baking powder
- 1 cup milk

◊ Take half of the batter out.

◊ Mix in mix master.

Get 3 tablespoons cocoa and mix into half of batter. Pour half of regular batter into pan (vegetable shortening) and then half of cocoa batter and then again half of regular batter and finally rest of cocoa batter. Bake at 325° oven for an hour.

POUND CAKE

- 10 large eggs
- 4 cups flour
- 1 lb. butter
- 3 1/2 cups sugar
- 1 teaspoon vanilla extract

Cream, sugar, butter, and eggs one at a time.

3-4 quick dashes of mace. Put into a tube pan (vegetable shortening)

Mix with mix master. Bake at 325° for 45 minutes and turn up to 350° for 45 minutes.

BANANA CAKE

- 2 1/2 cups flour
- 2 1/2 teaspoons baking powder
- 1/2 teaspoon baking soda
- 1/2 teaspoon salt
- 1/2 cup shortening (8 tablespoons)
- 1 teaspoon vanilla extract
- 1 1/4 cup sugar
- 2 large eggs
- 1/4 cup milk

1 cup mashed bananas (2). Cream shortening. Add sugar and eggs one at a time into mix master. Add vanilla. Finally, add dry ingredients into milk and bananas. Bake at 375° oven for 30 minutes.

CREAM CHEESE POUND CAKE

- 1/2 lb. softened butter

- 8 oz softened cream cheese

- 1 1/2 cups sugar

- 1 1/2 teaspoons vanilla extract

- 2 cups flour

- 1 1/2 teaspoon baking powder

- 4 large eggs

Beat butter and cheese together until blended in mix master. Beat in sugar, vanilla until fluffy. Add one egg at a time. Add flour. Add baking powder and blend into beaten mixture. Pour batter into a loaf pan lined with wax paper or brown bag. Bake at 325° for 1 hr. 10 minutes.

SOUR CREAM POUND

- 2 3/4 cups sugar

- 3 sticks butter, softened

- 6 large eggs, one at a time

- 1 teaspoon vanilla extract

- 3 cups flour

- 1 orange rind-zested, don't go down to white

- 1 teaspoon baking powder

- 1/2 teaspoon salt

- 1 cup sour cream

Use a tube pan (vegetable shortening). Use mix master. Bake at 350° for 55-65 mins.

SOUR CREAM CAKE

- 1 cup butter

- 3 cups sugar

- 6 large eggs

- 1/2-pint sour cream

- 3 cups flour

- 3 teaspoons baking powder

- 1/4 teaspoon salt

Beat for ten minutes. (butter, sugar and cream) with mix master.

Add 1 teaspoon baking soda and 2 teaspoons of vanilla or almond extract and beat again. Put half of batter into greased tube pan. Get 2 tablespoons of cinnamon and a half cup of regular sugar and mix. Pour on top of half batter and then add rest of batter. Bake at 325° for 1 1/2 hrs.

RICE RICOTTA PIE

- 3 lb. ricotta
- 2 teaspoons flour
- 1 tablespoon vanilla extract
- 1/2 teaspoon salt
- 2 cups sugar
- 9 large eggs
- 2 blocks of Philadelphia Cream Cheese (softened)
- 1 cup of cooked rice (Carolina)
- 1 can evaporated milk

Square pan, coat with vegetable shortening. Beat ingredients with hand mixer. Bake at 325° for 1 hour.

CREAM CHEESE COOKIES

- 1 cup butter
- 2 cups flour
- 1 cup sugar
- 8 oz cream cheese
- 2 egg yolks
- 1/2 teaspoon salt
- 1 teaspoon vanilla extract

   *Can add crushed walnuts or pecans. *

Dough will be thick. Mix by hand. Use teaspoon to put globs of dough onto greased cookie tray.

   Bake for 12 -15 minutes at 400°.

OATMEAL COOKIES

- 3 cups oatmeal

- 1 cup flour

- 3/4 teaspoon salt

- 1/2 teaspoon baking soda

- 4 tablespoons melted butter

- 1/2 cup oil

- 1/4 teaspoon cinnamon

- 3/4 cup brown sugar

- 1/2 cup regular sugar

- One whole egg and one yolk

- 1 teaspoon vanilla extract

◊   Mix by hand.

   *You can add a half cup of raisins. *

Use a tablespoon to put mix onto pan. Bake at 375° for 10 minutes.

CHOCOLATE CHIP TEA CAKES (COOKIES)

- 2 sticks butter, softened

- 1/2 cup powdered sugar

- 1 teaspoon vanilla extract

- 2 cups flour

- *2/3 cup chopped nuts if you want

- 2 cups of semi-sweet chocolate morsels (chips)

Beat butter and powdered sugar until creamy by hand.

Add in vanilla. Gradually beat in flour and nuts.

Stir in the morsels. Roll into one-inch balls. Place onto greased baking sheet. Bake at 350° for 10-12 minutes or until light golden brown on bottom.

HAMANTASH

- 1 cup oil

- 1 cup sugar

- 2 large eggs

- 4 cups flour (judge-start with 3-you want a dry dough, not real dry)

- 2 teaspoons baking powder

- 1 teaspoon vanilla extract

- dash salt

- 1/2 cup orange juice

Roll dough flat to about 1/8-inch thickness. Use a drinking glass to cut circles. Get prune or plum paste. Put about a half teaspoon into middle. Then pinch left and right side and top and bottom. It should look like a triangle. Grease a cookie sheet with vegetable shortening. Bake at 350° for 18 minutes.

BOW TIES

- 5 egg yolks
- 3 tablespoons sugar
- 5 tablespoons sour cream
- 1 tablespoon lemon juice
- 2 1/2 cups flour
- 1/4 teaspoon salt
- 1 teaspoon baking powder
- 2 tablespoons of rum or blackberry brandy

Beat eggs, sugar. Stir in sour cream, brandy/rum, and lemon juice. Mix flour, salt, and baking powder. It should be soft dough. Work the dough on a floured surface. Roll thin and cut into strips (use a cutter with ruffled edge) about 4 inches long and an inch wide. You can tie or pinch in the middle to make your bow ties. Put them into deep fryer until golden brown. Add powder sugar or honey when cooled.

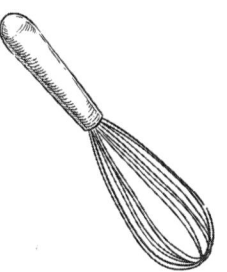

HOT CROSS BUNS

- 1 cup sugar

- 1 teaspoon salt

- 1 cup butter

- 2 large eggs

- 3 packs yeast

- 1 cup of raisins

- 8 1/2 cups flour (judge-dough should be sticky)

- 1/3 cup of orange rind, no white

- 2 cups milk

- Citron optional

Combine the sugar, salt, yeast and 2 cups of flour. Over a low heat, warm milk, and butter. With a hand mixer on low speed gradually beat the liquid ingredients with the dry ingredients. You can then increase the speed and beat in the eggs and two more cups of flour. Continue beating and then knead in the rest of the flour which is about 4 1/2 cups. Add in your orange rind and raisins, it should feel elastic. Shape the dough into a huge ball and place into a bowl that has butter rubbed onto all sides- let it rise -in about one hour.

Now divide your dough into pieces and shape into hot cross buns. The mixture should make approximately 24 buns. Brush each one with egg yolk and water mixture.

Bake at 350° for 25-30 minutes on a cookie pan (Vegetable shortening). After cooled, mix 3/4 cup of powdered sugar, a tablespoon of milk, 1/3 teaspoons lemon juice and water until frosting like consistency and make cross shape on top.

BLACK DEVILS

*Walnuts (optional-judge for yourself) *

- 2 1/2 cups sugar

- 1 teaspoon baking powder

- 1 teaspoon baking soda

- 2 large eggs

- pinch salt

- 3/4 cup milk

- 4 cups flour

- 4 tablespoons of cocoa

Put cocoa into 1/4 cup of milk on a stove along with a 1/2 teaspoon of oil. Cool it. Add eggs and then dry ingredients into mix master. Make into a loaf on cookie pan (vegetable shortening). Bake at 375° for 15 minutes. When done, cut the same as biscotti's, approximately one inch wide.

CHEESE CUPCAKES

- 3- 8-ounce blocks of Philly Cream Cheese

- 1 cup sugar

- 1 1/2 teaspoon vanilla extract

- 5 large eggs

◊   Mix well with mix master. Put into cup cake pan into cupcake paper.

◊   Bake for 40 minutes on 300°. Let cool.

Topping-1 cup of sour cream, 1/4 cup sugar, 1/4 teaspoon vanilla extract. Mix by hand. Should be like an icing consistency. Place only the cherry, the one from the pie filling brand, on top. Put back into oven for 5-10 minutes.

CREME PUFFS

- 1/2 cup vegetable shortening in a pot with 1 cup water-boil.

Grab 1 cup of flour and a teaspoon of salt. Beat mixture with a wooden spoon into the vegetable shortening and water when boiling. Keep stirring until thick. Take off heat. Get 4 large eggs, beat good, one at a time into the dough. Mix should be smooth. Get a greased cookie sheet. Grab dough with a tablespoon and put onto cookie sheet (about 2 inches apart) and bake at 450° for 25 minutes. Let them get cold and cut the top off and fill with Italian creme and place top back on. You can remove the dough inside to get more creme in.

ITALIAN CREAM

- 1 quart of milk
- 8 tablespoons corn starch
- 1 3/4 cup sugar
- 4 tablespoons butter
- 4 large eggs
- 1 teaspoon vanilla extract

Cook on stove in a double broiler (pot w water inside pot w ingredients) until thick. When cool, add light rum (judge). Approximately a shot, maybe a little more.

ICE BOX CAKE

Arrange graham crackers on bottom of dish. Make vanilla pudding and pour onto graham crackers. Put another layer of graham cracker and now make chocolate pudding and pour on top of crackers. Stick in fridge until it hardens. Add maraschino cherries or whipped cream when you serve.

NO NAME ITALIAN DONUT

- 4 large eggs

- 1 cup of honey

- 1 cup oil

- 1/2 teaspoon anise oil

- anise (judge)

- 2 tablespoons baking powder

- about 4 cups baking flour

Mix by hand. Roll 2 long strings about 1/2 inch wide by 6 inches long. Plat them and then make a circle and pinch it closed when you have a circle.

Get powdered sugar and milk-mix together until an icing consistency. Not too thick, not too thin. As soon as you remove donuts from oven, dip into the icing. Let sit on wax paper.

Bake at 350° for 20 minutes

BUTTER CREAM EASTER EGG

- 1/2 lb. butter (room temp)

- 1 lb. 10x powdered sugar. Add more if needed.

- 1 teaspoon vanilla extract

- 2/3 cup sweetened milk

Mix by hand. *You can add pecan or fruit (dried fruit). * Refrigerate for hour. Form into egg shape. Should be pasty, sticky. Put in fridge to cool. Remove and dip into chocolate with a fork. (Get a large bag of milk chocolate or dark chocolate chips and melt. Add some oil.) Put on wax paper to dry.

COCONUT EASTER EGGS

- 1-8 oz cream cheese
- 1/4 lb. butter
- 2 -13-ounce bags of shredded, sweetened coconut
- 1 teaspoon vanilla extract
- 1 lb. 10 x powdered sugar. Add if you need more.

Mix by hand. Form into egg shape. Refrigerate for an hour, shape into eggs. Refrigerate again for 2-3 hours. Dip in chocolate of your liking. Put on wax paper to dry.

PIZZELLES

- 6 large eggs
- 2 cups flour
- 1 cup sugar
- 1 cup vegetable oil
- anise seeds (tablespoon) or anise oil (half teaspoon)

Mix by hand or mix master-watch for lumps.

*When you roll pizzelle and put small piece of Hershey chocolate in center, don't use anise oil, use 1 tablespoon of vanilla extract in mix. *

** Need a pizzelle iron to make above**

ALL cakes and cookies go into a pre heated oven EXCEPT the Small 9th Street Pound

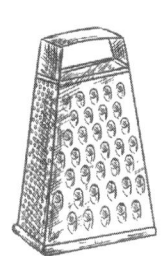 # Dishes

MANICOTTI SHELLS

- 4 large eggs

- 2 tablespoons of melted butter

- 2 cups flour

- 2 cups milk

- 1 teaspoon salt

Mix with mix master. Get lumps out. Get a small frying pan, approximately 4-6 inches in diameter. Grease pan with butter and once melted, dump excess out. Start making crepes by adding a little bit of batter. Rotate the pan until the batter forms around the pan in shape of circle. Cook for maybe 20 seconds and then flip to cook other side.

Make the crepes cool before you stuff with ricotta. Make 3 lbs. of ricotta, 2 eggs, 1/2 cup macaroni cheese, salt, parsley. Fill manicotti and roll. Put into a pan, add your gravy. Cover with aluminum foil. Bake at 350° for 35-45 minutes.

CIAMBOTTA

- 6 large potatoes peeled and diced.

- 1 medium yellow onion, sliced.

Add potato and yellow onion into a pot and fry (don't brown) with oil for 5 minutes, no lid. Get a can of crushed tomato (add salt, oregano, parsley, basil) and pour into pan with potatoes. Add 2 green zucchinis, sliced (leave some of the skin) along with a small pack of sliced mushrooms and 2 red bell peppers, sliced. You can add more crushed tomato, you must judge if more is needed.

Cook with lid on. Use low to medium heat until fork easily goes into potato (approximately 30-45 minutes) Last 10-15 mins, cut 4 hot dogs up and throw in, uncooked. If the sauce looks too thick you can add a little bit of water.

CABBAGE

Chop a head of cabbage up. Fry 3 strips of bacon, cut up, in oil. Put 2 fresh tomatoes in, cut up. Throw in sliced mushrooms. Add cabbage with water and let cook until cabbage is soft. Approximately 35 minutes. Salt/black pepper to taste.

STUFFED CABBAGE

Boil whole head of cabbage. Take out and peel each leaf off gently. Get ground pork and boiled rice. Mix like a meatball. Eggs, macaroni cheese, garlic, salt, pepper, parsley and roll leaves. Place into a pan. Have a can of crushed tomato and make a marinara sauce. Fry oil and garlic, add the crushed tomato and parsley, salt, oregano. Now put marinara sauce on top of cabbage. Cover with aluminum foil and bake at 350° for 50 minutes to an hour.

MACARONI PIE

- 1 lb. of bucatini (thick spaghetti) Boil.

Beat 10 eggs in separate bowl. A cup of macaroni cheese. Cut soppressata into diced chunks. Lots of black pepper. Mix. Put in square pan greased with butter. Put bread crumb on top (sprinkle) and 4,5 pats of butter. Bake in oven 350° for 30 minutes.

SHRIMP AND SPAGHETTI

- 12-16 medium sized shrimp

- 4 cloves of garlic

- basil, oregano, salt, and pepper

- Bag of baby spinach

- 1/2 lemon, squeezed

- grated macaroni cheese

- 1 lb. spaghetti

In a pan put 2 tablespoons of oil and 2 tablespoons of butter. Add shrimp, basil, oregano, salt, and pepper and four cloves of garlic and a tablespoon of hot pepper flakes. Sauté in the pan for 10 minutes. Meanwhile boil your pasta, drain, then throw in with shrimp. Add 4 tablespoons of butter, 1/2 lemon juice and cheese. Toss.

GRAVY

- 4 cans of crushed tomato.

Salt, pepper, basil, teaspoon of sugar. Put on medium heat. Once it starts to boil/splash, put on low heat.

Mix 2 lb. ground meat mix (beef, pork, veal) with 2 eggs, tablespoon crushed garlic, 1/2 cup macaroni cheese and bread crumb (judge), parsley until able to form a meatball. Fry meatballs in oil along with a pound of sweet and a pound of hot sausage. Have an onion and 2 garlic cloves in pan while frying. Place cooked meat into gravy. Toss onion after frying is complete. Add a large splash of the oil you were frying your meat in into the gravy, stir occasionally. Cook for about 2-3 hours on low to medium heat with lid half on. You can also get small pieces of beef pork and veal, fry them up and put into the gravy.

CRAB GRAVY

Get a dozen small to medium size blue point crabs. Make sure backs are removed and they are clean. Place into a large pot with oil and garlic. Season with parsley, salt, pepper, red pepper flakes if you like spicy. Cover with lid. When they turn orange, they are done. Now add in about 5 cans of crushed tomato. Season again. Cook for about 2 hours on low heat, stirring occasionally, with lid half on. Make spaghetti al dente and add the crab gravy.

TUNA GRAVY

- 1 can of Italian tuna
- 3 cloves of garlic
- 1 can of paste and 1 can of crushed tomato

Put oil in a pot and let it get hot. Place tuna in and brown for about 7 minutes. Get a tablespoon of paste and brown for another 5 minutes. Add a Bermuda (purple) onion and garlic, both sliced thin, for another 5 minutes until brown. Put in a can of crushed tomato and a 1/4 can of water. Add oregano, black pepper, parsley, and salt. Cook for 1 and 1/2 hours. Gas not too high, on low to medium. Cook with lid half on.

MARINARA

Get a couple cloves of garlic and fry in olive oil. Add a can or two of plum tomatoes and squeeze by hand. Season with parsley, salt, basil, and pepper. Cook for about 20 minutes with lid half on.

STRING BEANS AND POTATOES IN GRAVY

Fresh string beans, boil for 5 minutes. Make sure you remove the ends. Remove skin and dice potatoes and put into pot of oil with a cut up, medium yellow onion. Let cool for 5 minutes but stir. Get a can of crushed tomato and dump in. Add some water, maybe a half of can. Get string beans and throw in. Let it cook together until potatoes are soft. Judge. You can add a half stick of thin, sliced pepperoni or one piece of fried, hot Italian sausage, with casing removed and meat cut up/crumbled.

ROASTED RED PEPPERS-COLD

Get red bell peppers-put in broiler, until black. Turn again until other side is black. Put them in a brown paper bag until cold. It helps to get the black off. Take black off and seeds out. Put on paper towel. Slice thin. Then fix. Add vegetable oil, salt, parsley and a lot of minced garlic.

SQUASH N EGGS

Fry green squash (or yellow) with a yellow onion in oil. Use a potato peeler and remove most, not all the skin. When squash is soft, add beaten eggs and dump into the squash and oil.

PORK N BEANS

Use 2, one-pound bags of Navy beans-wash and soak overnight. Cover beans with water. Throw water away. Put clean water in beans, about an inch over them and boil for one hour. Get a 4 lb. roast pork (seasoned) and grab beans with the water and dump all (water too) into a roasting pan. Use 2 large bottles of ketchup, a half teaspoon of white vinegar and 2 wooden spoons of dark corn syrup and mix. Bake at 350°, uncovered for an hour, hour, and a half. Stir occasionally. Cover after about an hour and a half. Let cook for another 3 1/2, 4 hrs. with lid.

STUFFED ITALIAN FRYING (CUBANELLES) PEPPER

Make filling with slice bread. You must judge how much bread to use depending on number of peppers. Wet the bread, squeeze out excess water. Put macaroni cheese, diced, fresh garlic, parsley, salt, pepper and an egg into bread and mix. Stuff the peppers with the mix. Put peppers into a frying pan with oil. Cook on low to medium heat. Brown a little on all sides. While cooking, add some splashes of Worcestershire sauce in.

TURKEY CUTLETS

Season them with black pepper and salt. Dredge them in flour and then egg whites, finally bread crumb. Fry in olive oil and butter over medium heat. Throw out most of the oil and butter. Now add about a cup of chicken stock and a can of crushed tomatoes and bring to a boil. Transfer everything into a bake pan and grate Parmesan cheese or provolone over the top. Bake at 450° for 10 minutes.

SPAGHETTI ALLA PUTTANESCA

Get a pint of cherry tomatoes and cut them in half. Season with salt, pepper, olive oil and oregano. Put them in a 400° oven for 20 minutes. In a frying pan, put olive oil and about five anchovies (place capers on side) on high heat. Heat them until the fish breaks down. Lower heat and add about three cloves of crushed garlic, capers, and hot pepper flakes. Cook spaghetti. When al dente, remove and put into a pan with chopped Kalamata olives. Add some of the pasta water and top with the tomatoes from the oven.

CHICKEN GIZZARDS

Cut approximately 2 pound of chicken gizzards small and fry in oil until water (when cooking, gizzards release water) evaporates. Cook till brown. If too much water, drain. Add oregano parsley and black pepper, garlic powder and salt. Add crushed tomatoes and cook until the gizzards soften. This takes approximately an hour.

PESTO ALLA GENOVESE

- Two cloves of garlic
- Two cups of fresh basil
- One cup parsley
- Half cup of grated cheese
- Half cup Romano cheese
- Twelve blackened almonds (boiled)
- One tablespoon of pignoli nuts
- Six walnuts (boiled)
- 3 tablespoons butter
- Half cup olive oil

*Grind in blender. Cook fettuccine. Add about four tablespoons of macaroni water and mix.

CHICKEN NEAPOLITAN

Fryer chicken cutlets and oil approximately five minutes (until cooked). Discard the grease. Add crushed garlic and parsley and return to heat. Stir in to pick up the flavors. Remove from heat and add a can of mushrooms. Add salt, pepper, parsley, oregano to taste. Throw in about five pats of butter and return to heat until melted. Eat with side of rice or pasta.

FETTUCCINE WITH SHRIMP

- One yellow onion
- One pound of shrimp
- One clove garlic
- Red pepper flakes
- One can of cherry tomatoes
- One tablespoon sugar
- Half cup red wine
- Basil
- Olive oil

Olive oil. Sauté garlic and hot pepper. Throw in the shrimp. Then throw in the tomatoes, sugar, basil, and wine. Cook for an hour, hour, and 10 minutes.

TRIPE

Soak 5 lb. tripe in salt and water for 15-20 minutes. Cut "stuff" from sides (underneath). Rinse good. Check for hairs and cut them out. Cut up tripe into bite size pieces. It will shrink when you cook. Boil for 15-20 mins. Dump water. Get oil, a big onion and a lot of celery and tripe placing everything into a pot. You can add a red bell pepper. Fry it up for about 5 minutes. Then add one can of crushed tomato. Half cup of red wine. Add some water. If more tomato is needed, add. Season with salt, pepper, a little bit of oregano, parsley, basil (no garlic powder). Cook on stove top for 2 1/2 to 3 hrs. turning so it doesn't stick. If gravy is too thick, add water.

PASTA FAGIOLI

Red (kidney) or white (cannellini) beans-do red with homemade macaroni. White you make with ditalini. Fry oil and garlic. Put beans in. Season with salt, pepper, parsley and a dash or basil and oregano. Cook for 5 minutes. While doing this boil water and cook ditalini until al dente. Drain macaroni but keep about a cup of the water and add to the beans.

PEAS AND MACARONI (PASTA AND PEAS)

Sauté yellow onion and oil and tomato paste (small can). Put about a half cup of red wine in. Put can of peas in. Cook 5 minutes. Season with salt, pepper, oregano, and parsley. Cook macaroni al dente. Keep cup of macaroni water. Use small shell type macaroni.

STRACCIATELLA

Make chicken soup. (Oil, 2 chopped carrots, 2 stalks celery sliced, medium onion diced-fry it up for a few mins. Put a whole, small three-to-four-pound chicken in pot. Add a small chicken broth and add water until chicken is covered.) Let cook for about an hour and a half, two hours, until chicken is cooked. A slow boil, covered with lid. Season with salt, pepper, parsley, and marjoram. When it's done, remove chicken from pot. Cut it up and place the diced meat back into the pot. Add 2 to 3 bags of baby leaf spinach and cooked orzo or rice (judge). When spinach cooks (2 minutes), let it come to a boil and then add 3 beaten eggs, stir then cover. Serve with macaroni cheese.

CAVATELLI WITH BROCCOLI RABE

Clean broccoli, remove from stems. Cut small. Fry in oil and garlic until cooked. Cover with lid. Boil water and drop in cavatelli. Remove. Keep some of the pasta water and combine with the broccoli rabe. You can also make with hot sausage. You would have to fry the sausage first with the garlic and then add the broccoli rabe into the same pan.

ESCAROLE AND BEANS

Clean escarole in water and salt. Cut into small pieces. Boil for about 5 minutes. Drain water. Fry oil and garlic. Put escarole in. Add large can of chicken broth and water. Let it cook until fork easily goes through the greens. The last five minutes, add a can of cannellini beans. Season with salt and pepper.

STUFFED EGGPLANT

Cut eggplant in half. Scoop inside of eggplant out. Boil the scooped-out eggplant until fork easily goes in. Drain. Get a pound of ground pork and about a cup of cooked rice, an egg, macaroni cheese, salt, black pepper, parsley and chopped garlic. Mix. Get eggplant halves and fill each with the mixture. Put some crushed tomato gravy on top of the mixture. Put some crushed tomato gravy on top of the mixture. Place eggplant onto oiled pan. Add some macaroni cheese on top. Cover with aluminum foil or a lid and bake on 350° for approximately 40 minutes.

SEAFOOD AND SPAGHETTI

Fry oil and garlic first. Add calamari (cut up or purchase the rings, can also use the tentacles), large shrimp, baby sea scallops and a can of crab meat. Fry for about 5 minutes. Add a can of crushed tomatoes along with a 1/4 to 1/2 can of water. Season with a little oregano, parsley, salt, pepper, and basil. Bring to a boil. Cook for 40 minutes on medium heat. Place on top of spaghetti.

MIXED SEAFOOD SALAD

- 1 can of scungilli-rinse good-cut small
- 2 lb. small bay scallops
- 2 lb. medium shrimp
- 1 lb. cut up calamari (or rings)

Boil each seafood separately until done (few minutes). Mix. Squeeze 2 lemons, zest a lemon, 1 teaspoon of white vinegar, vegetable oil, salt, pepper, hot pepper flakes and chopped celery. Mix. Put in fridge until chilled.

BEEF BARLEY SOUP

- 1 1/2 lbs. London Broil
- Soup bone

Cut your London Broil into small pieces. Chop an onion, celery, and carrots up. Put everything into a pot and add some oil and fry until meat is brown. Cook for a few minutes and then add a can of beef broth and 2 cups of water. Add in a half cup of barley. You can also chop up some spinach and add into your pot. Cook for about 1 1/2 to 2 hours on low to medium heat with lid on.

ESCAROLE SOUP (WEDDING SOUP)

Make chicken soup. (Oil, 2 chopped carrots, 2 stalks celery sliced, medium onion diced-fry it up for a few mins. Put a whole, small three-to-four-pound chicken in pot. Add a small chicken broth and add water until chicken is covered.) Get ground meat (mix with garlic, macaroni cheese, salt, pepper, parsley, one egg) and make mini meatballs. Put into soup raw. Bring to a boil. Drop meatballs in. Reduce heat to low, medium. Clean and part boil escarole. Remove and strain. When soup is finished in about an hour, add escarole. Let cook together for another 5 minutes.

TUNA SALAD WITH CANNELLINI BEANS

- 2 cans of Italian Tuna
- 1 can of Cannellini beans, strain out the juice

Chop up celery, carrots and yellow onion, red pepper flakes.

Mix everything together, adding some olive oil. Chill and serve cold.

BUCATINI ALL' AMATRICIANA

- 2 tablespoons olive oil

- 4 ounces pancetta or bacon

- 1/3 teaspoon crushed red pepper flakes

- 3/4 cup minced onion

- Slice some garlic, judge

- 1 can of crushed tomato

- Kosher salt

- Grated cheese

Heat oil on medium heat. Add pancetta and cook until crisp (about 4 minutes). Add red pepper flakes and black pepper. Add garlic and onions, cooking until soft (about 8 minutes). Add tomatoes and then reduce heat to low. Cook 20-25 minutes. Save a cup of pasta water. Add pasta water to skillet along with the pasta. Stir in the cheese.

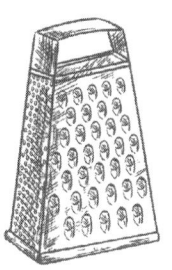